BEAT
THE
MIDDLE

PQO520036

The Middle School Student's Guide to Academic Success

$0.95 = 95\%$

$a^2 + b^2 = c^2$

BLAKE & BO NEMELKA

BEAT
THE
MIDDLE

The Middle School Student's Guide to Academic Success

BLAKE & BO NEMELKA

Beat the Middle: The Middle School Student's Guide to Academic Success
Copyright © 2014 Blake & Bo Nemelka
ISBN Number: 978-0-9960693-0-4
Product of Nemelka Group, LLC

www.beatthemiddle.com
info@beatthemiddle.com

Website & Design: Alex Kolody Design
Editor: Marianna Larsen
Layout, Design, & Printing: Book Printers of Utah, Inc.

*To all middle school students
and their parents/mentors...*

TABLE OF CONTENTS

INTRODUCTION

If you are a student reading this book, we commend you. You are awesome! You have taken the first and perhaps most important step to academic success. You want it and are seeking guidance on how to achieve it. We believe this book will be an excellent guide for you; however, you will need help from someone to understand parts of it. Also, there are sections that require someone to hold you accountable to the action items we will invite you to complete. We wrote this book to challenge you, but we do not want you to be discouraged or give up. You can do this! Please ask dependable people in your life to read this book with you and help you along the way. We refer to these individuals as parents/mentors. They are all around you—in your family, school, and community.

If you are a parent/mentor of a student reading this book, we commend you as well. You are invested in a student's academic success and are seeking ways to help. We believe this book will prepare you to do just that. Let's be honest, the majority of middle school students will not read this book alone; therefore, we invite you to read the chapters, understand the content, and hold students accountable to the action items. If you force this book onto students, it won't work. Our solution for you to engage students in this material is to find ways to inspire them to want academic success. We can't do this for you because you know the students best, but we are confident you will feel prompted and guided as you put time and attention into helping them succeed. As you do this, remember these words by William Arthur Ward, "The mediocre teacher tells. The good teacher explains. The superior teacher demonstrates. The great teacher inspires."

This book discusses 12 factors of academic success, and each is written in the form of a conversation. We carefully chose the word "conversation" because we want students and parents/mentors to be engaged in a dialogue with us and with each other. For this reason, each conversation is structured as such:

- **Listen** to what the factor is and why it's important

- **Learn** from the examples of others

- **Reflect** upon your answers to thought-provoking questions

- **Act** by completing the provided template

As you engage in the 12 conversations together, do not overlook the valuable contributions of others. It certainly takes a village to raise a child. For example, we have many people who have supported us and continue to support us in our academic pursuits including spouses, parents, stepparents, siblings, in-laws, friends, aunts and uncles, grandparents, cousins, religious leaders, teachers, counselors, coaches, etc. These are our parents/mentors.

We remember when we were in the Boy Scouts of America and certain skills were required to earn a merit badge—a symbol representing the scout had learned a specific skill. Someone trained in his or her field taught each merit badge class. Parents/mentors can learn from this model by connecting students with those more qualified than themselves in select areas. You'll be grateful for and surprised at the talent that exists in your family, community, and even online.

Achieving academic success is a process. In order for you to better understand this process, we built an Academic Success Model. Parents/mentors should realize that most students are not going to take the initiative to learn and apply the elements of this model; thus, it is parents/mentors who must be disciplined and hold students accountable to this process. Students may not always express it, but they depend on their parents/mentors for support. Students need parents/mentors who are hands-on and committed to helping them for years to come.

From this point on, we will speak directly to students because this book is for them. We feel students are more likely to take personal ownership of their academic success if directly invited to do so through a conversational approach. Let the conversations begin....

ACADEMIC SUCCESS MODEL

As we look back on our middle school years, we are reminded of how difficult, yet how important, they were. You're not a child, but you're also not an adult. While this age can be challenging, it is one of the most important times in your life because you are laying the foundation for your academic success.

We know you have desires to succeed in school and try really hard, but do you ever feel like you can't seem to get ahead? Do you feel average? This feeling occurs because academic success is thought of as earning A's, whereas most students earn some A's but have a C average. Below is a curve that represents middle school grades in general.

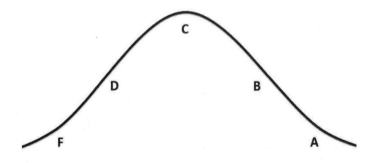

This curve is low on the left, high in the middle, and low on the right, showing you that some students average F's and D's, most students are in the middle with a C average, and other students average B's and A's. We certainly agree grades are important, but other factors should be considered when thinking about your academic success, including:

1. Goals and Mentors

2. Planning and Preparation

3. Time Management

4. GPA

5. College Entrance Exams

6. Internships and Work Experience

7. Extra- and Co-Curricular Activities

8. Service

9. Money Management and Scholarships

10. The Application Process

11. Interviewing

12. Giving Back

If you do not learn and apply these 12 factors, you will feel stuck in the middle of trying hard to achieve academic success. There is a process to beating the middle! This process is founded upon four principles that you can follow to guide your journey to academic success—now and through high school.

Four Guiding Principles:

1. Desire

You **want** to succeed academically through being inspired by someone you trust.

Imagine someone giving you a delicious apple which he/she grew, inspiring you to plant the apple seeds yourself and grow your own delicious apples.

2. Act

You learn and **try** implementing the 12 factors.

You plant the apple seeds and give them water, sunlight, and nutrients. Through these actions you begin to see a plant grow—short-term evidence that what you are doing is working.

3. Endure

You consistently **do** what the 12 factors require over time.

You diligently and patiently nourish the plant into a tree over a long period of time with confidence that your consistent actions will produce results— delicious apples.

4. Achieve

You accomplish your original desire and **share** your experiences to help others achieve their potential.

Your tree produces delicious apples you can pick, eat, and share with someone who you feel would benefit and be able to grow their own delicious apples.

These four guiding principles, together with learning and applying the 12 factors over time, can be summarized in an Academic Success Model, as seen below. We've drawn arrows around each principle to represent a continuous process that instills desire, invites action, encourages endurance, and rewards achievement over time. As you follow the four guiding principles and are held accountable for learning and applying the 12 factors taught in this book, you will beat the middle and help others do the same.

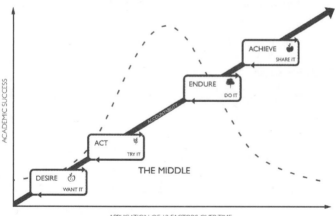

CONVERSATION 1:
GOALS AND MENTORS

"When a young person, even a gifted one, grows up without proximate living examples of what she may aspire to become—whether lawyer, scientist, artist, or leader in any realm—her goal remains abstract. Such models as appear in books or on the news, however inspiring or revered, are ultimately too remote to be real, let alone influential. But a role model in the flesh provides more than inspiration; his or her very existence is confirmation of possibilities one may have every reason to doubt, saying, 'Yes, someone like me can do this."

—*Supreme Court Justice Sonia Sotomayor*

LISTEN. We do not expect you to make a decision today concerning the rest of your life. That is not the purpose of this conversation. In fact, goals change so frequently that we need to understand the idea of having them set and yet being flexible to change. However, there is one extremely important concept that you must know, and you have probably heard this before. You need to write down your goals! There is power in writing down your goals because they are direct reflections of your desires. When we write down a goal, our mind is better able to commit it to memory because it took thought and action.

When formulating your goals, including as much detail as possible is important; however, we care most about actually writing the goals down. So if all you have as a goal is "go to college," then we can work with that. Writing down something like "go to a top-20 college by the time I'm nineteen years old" is, of course, a better, more defined goal, but we need to start with the basics.

You are going to have goals for several aspects of your life. Earning good grades in high school, scoring well on the ACT/SAT, and attending college are great academic goals for you to consider, but be sure to think about everything that makes you unique. Do you want to play an instrument or practice a sport? Do you want to save a certain amount of money to buy something special? Each day you should have certain tasks or goals that you would like to accomplish. This is your "to-do" list, right?

We will talk more about daily, weekly, and even monthly goals in *Conversation 3: Time Management;* nevertheless, it is important to think about time frames as you formulate goals. When looking into the future, excluding short-term goals, we believe you should have, at minimum, goals laid out for the next six months, one year, three years, and five years.

Now, we need to talk about your parents/mentors. A parent/mentor is someone whom you go to with questions about life. Having parents/mentors has many benefits. For example, they may recognize potential in you that you do not recognize in yourself. Secondly, you need to be encouraged by others to accomplish your goals. And last, but certainly not least, you must reach out to others who have specific skills and experiences to coach you towards success.

You most likely will have a combination of parents/mentors, but having goal-specific parents/mentors to whom you are accountable is important. Give them a copy of your goals and get together often to review them. Tell your parents/mentors why you chose them to help you. They will be honored to feel your love for them and will be diligent in holding you accountable for the goals you share together. No matter the person, be sure you always have at least one parent/mentor with whom you check in with on a weekly basis. Also, be sure this parent/mentor is honest with you about your progress towards the accomplishment of your goals.

Never underestimate the power of friendship. Some of the most influential people in our lives have been our middle school friends. We went through the same grades together and helped each other along the way. You are influenced by whom you hang out with. Having good friends will make you a better person. Having friends who don't have your best interests at heart will pull you down. Choose your friends wisely.

LEARN. In middle school we started a friendship with Ted. Ted is well-respected in our family because of what he did in eighth grade. Ted struggled with obesity throughout childhood and into middle school. His weight never got to the point that he couldn't be active, but we could definitely tell he was unhappy with his appearance. At such a young age, this weight was detrimental both physically and psychologically. This all changed one summer day. We're not sure what happened exactly, but Ted set a goal to lose weight. He was sick of the way he looked and felt inside, and instead of researching intense dieting plans or quick weight-loss routines, he set a goal to run daily.

On the first day he left his house, he started his run to the nearest stop sign. Doing so nearly made him pass out, but that was his goal, and he did it! Running to the end of the street is something he had never done before, and being outdoors in front of neighbors required tremendous confidence. With the help of his parents/mentors, Ted ran to the stop sign each day until he felt comfortable running a longer distance. Over the course of a year, Ted dropped all his extra weight and became one of the most physically fit kids in school. In fact, Ted was able to join a competitive marching band and also became one of our high school's best cross-country runners. If you had told us in eighth grade that Ted would become one of our school's best athletes, we would not have believed you. Ted's determination is commendable, and he is proof that a young person can set and achieve major goals.

Ted's story is inspiring and is one of many examples of students who desire change and achieve it through goal setting and hard work. We have seen family and friends overcome illness, earn perfect grades and test scores, build business empires, and help others through years of service to church and military organizations, to name a few. With the resources available to each of us through modern research and technology, we hardly ever hear the word "impossible" anymore. Whatever your goals are—now is the time to develop them further with the help of a parent/mentor. Do not wait until you are forced to think about something such as going to college. Imagine what opportunities will open up to you when looking for a great college having made the goals and taken the necessary steps to succeed years before applying.

REFLECT. Please take as much time as you need to ponder the following questions, and with the help of your parents/mentors, fill in your answers in the space provided.

What are the most important things you want to accomplish in life?

Get a good education & be happy

What six areas of life are the most important to you (school, family, church, etc.)?

family, friends, food, religion, School, home

What is unique about you?

I can't STAND having hair

What would be the first thing you would want to change about your life?

my hormones

Who are the three most influential people in your life and why?

my mom (mentor) My therapist (my support), my dad (challenges)

Where do you see yourself in six months, one year, three years, and five years?

6 - becoming a man   1- taking college courses
3 - having a steady relationship
5 - moving out

✝

CONVERSATION

Goals and Mentors

ACTION:

As you reflect upon the most important things in your life, please write down your top six goals and the people who will help you achieve each goal. Having lifelong goals will guide you in the years to come. Please make a copy of this action item to share with your parents/mentors.

Please visit www.beatthemiddle.com/act to download this template.

TOP SIX LIFELONG GOALS	PARENTS/MENTORS
1.	
2.	
3.	
4.	
5.	
6.	

Example on Back…

BEAT
THE
MIDDLE

GOALS AND MENTORS EXAMPLE:

TOP SIX LIFELONG GOALS	PARENTS/MENTORS
1. School: Graduate from college	Ms. Kinzer – English Teacher
2. Home: Have a happy family	My Parents
3. Work: Pursue a career I love	Aunt Swendy – Entrepreneur
4. Health: Live a healthy lifestyle	Jesse – My Running Partner
5. Service: Serve others daily	Sister Maureen – Religious Leader
6. Fun: Enjoy life!	Sam – My Best Friend

CONVERSATION 2:

PLANNING AND PREPARATION

"Another way to be prepared is to think negatively. Yes, I'm a great optimist. But, when trying to make a decision, I often think of the worst case scenario. I call it 'the eaten by wolves factor.' If I do something, what's the most terrible thing that could happen? Would I be eaten by wolves? One thing that makes it possible to be an optimist, is if you have a contingency plan for when all hell breaks loose. There are a lot of things I don't worry about, because I have a plan in place if they do."

—Randy Pausch

LISTEN. Now that we have gone through the process of setting goals, you need a period of reflection to plan the steps to accomplish your goals and to prepare yourself for anything that could happen as you execute your plan. Planning and preparation bridges the gap between goal establishment and time management, which we will discuss in Conversation 3.

One successful method of organizing your planning and preparation is to think about your life in six-month increments. Knowing what you want to do today and tomorrow and next week and next month is important, but true planning and preparation comes when you take several months at a time and set realistic benchmarks. For us, the benchmarks are the beginning of a new calendar year and the beginning of a new school year. These dates are natural breaking points with school being out, and they serve as great reflection times for what is to come in your life in the next half year, especially as it relates to your academic success. Six months has proven to be a sufficient amount of time for our brains to comprehend. This will become even more real for you when you go to college, because most college students are home in the summer and winter months and are in school during the fall and spring months.

The next step in properly planning and preparing for academic success is setting aside time for reflection, pondering, and meditation. The process of meditation looks differently for each person and occurs at different times of the day. Some people start their day reading and writing. Others think best while exercising or taking a shower. People have many ways of relaxing and thinking; however, allow us to share a few tips we believe can be successful for you.

First, wake up early! We could spend a lot of time showing you the hundreds of articles about this practice and how it will bring you success, but honestly, just try it, and you will realize why it is effective. Start today. Go to bed around 10:30 p.m. and set your alarm for 6 a.m. Spend the next hour in a set routine that consists of, but is not limited to, exercising, showering, reading, and writing. After you are done with those things, which should take about an hour, then you can finish getting ready for the day and go to school. Now, we already know what some of you are thinking, "Great idea, but that's not going to happen!" Well, we invite you to try it, and we promise you will learn to love the early morning hours more than any other time of your day because of how productive you will be.

Make a habit of thinking through your entire day during your morning routine. What do you need to be prepared for? Who are you going to run into? Is there anything you are forgetting, or are there opportunities that you haven't thought about yet? Starting your day in reflection and meditation is a remarkable way to achieve your goals because your mind and body are alert.

Having daily to-do lists is important. There is no right way of capturing your reminders, but most people use some sort of notepad or electronic app. You will think of several things during the morning and even throughout the day that you need to remember. Write them down. For example, if you know you have a presentation in your history class later in the day, and while in your morning routine you have the idea to play a certain video in your presentation, write it down. This will be a physical reminder to do it. Just like with goals, you will forget personal promptings unless you write them down. A running to-do list is essential for you to be as productive as possible, and, trust us, the majority of your best ideas will come in the early hours of the morning.

Writing down your thoughts is a concept that can translate to maintaining a great résumé—a document summarizing your academic, professional, and personal experiences. Let us explain a bit more. Too often we sit down to help someone with a résumé, and we begin with a blank sheet of paper or a new blank document on the computer. Having to go back through someone's life and remember everything worthy of including on a résumé is a time-consuming, painful process. We wish someone would have told him/her in middle school and high school, as you are learning now, to write everything down that would remotely be considered as something good for a résumé. Please start doing this. You don't need to have a perfect format. We will actually provide you a sheet to do this later in our conversation, and we encourage you to keep it updated frequently, both on the sheet and electronically. Doing this will help you because when you want to apply for a great after-school or summer job, you will not have to work on your application from scratch.

The last concept we want you to consider is the need to do more research while planning and preparing. Too many people decide they are going to do something without fully understanding all of the details or options. For example, when we got to the point of applying to colleges, we remember many friends of ours simply applying to the college closest to their home or to the college their family all attended. Some didn't even think about going to college after high school because nobody encouraged them to go, perhaps because many of them did not go themselves. Now this is just one example, but we could discuss many scenarios, such as picking which classes to take in school or where to work or what activities to get involved in. The point is this—do your research! Take an hour to look at your options and make a pros and cons list. Planning and preparing for your life is too important to leave up to spontaneous reaction. Remember, your parents/mentors can and should assist you with your research. Just ask them for help.

LEARN. The valedictorian of our high school class (out of 800+ graduating seniors) is named Bryce, and he happens to be one of our best friends. Bryce earned a perfect 4.0 GPA every quarter in school since the seventh grade, which means he brought home 24 perfect report cards before he graduated from high school. He is an amazing individual who understands what it means to plan and prepare. Bryce also finished high school with over 60 college credits; so in addition to his high school diploma, Bryce received his associate's degree and a scholarship to pretty much any college he wanted to attend without having to pay anything.

We never remember a time when Bryce came to class without having a finished assignment or without having read ahead in preparation for the day's lecture. Bryce has always been a little reserved. He wasn't a "know-it-all" student with his hand raised frequently, although he did ask questions when needed. Bryce simply understands the meaning of preparing and planning for the day. He had a routine and would think ahead. Bryce knew in seventh grade that his hard work would pay off later, and he started to build his résumé at an early age. He researched the teachers and classes at our school to find the right fit for his talents and aspirations. Often times we would find Bryce reading and pondering in meditation, which was easy to tell because he had a habit of eating paper when he was in full concentration mode! Was he "nerdy"? Yes, a little, and so were we, but that didn't mean that hobbies and friends and fun weren't part of life.

There's enough time for everything if you do not procrastinate and work hard. We learned a lot from Bryce about dedicating time to a goal and planning for the accomplishment of that goal. Bryce continues to teach us what it means to be smart and well-rounded. Some people are just plain gifted with intelligence, true, but you can teach yourself and learn to be smart with the right planning and preparation.

REFLECT. Please take as much time as you need to ponder the following questions, and with the help of your parents/mentors, fill in your answers in the space provided.

What do you need to plan and prepare for in the next six months?

A body exam and a positive attitude

What helps you think and meditate?

music

What would your ideal morning routine look like?

_get up, work out, shower, dress,
makeup_

How should you plan to accomplish your top six lifelong goals?

Careful planning, dedication, and positivity

How can your parents/mentors help you realize your goals?

Support

What types of decisions are you currently making without any research?

The decision to stand up for myself

CONVERSATION

Planning and Preparation

ACTION:

As you think about your six lifelong goals that you listed in the last conversation, begin to set specific plans for the accomplishment of your goals in the next six months and continually repeat this process.

Please visit www.beatthemiddle.com/act to download this template.

TOP SIX LIFELONG GOALS	SIX-MONTH PLAN
1.	
2.	
3.	
4.	
5.	
6.	

Example on Back...

PLANNING AND PREPARATION EXAMPLE:

TOP SIX LIFELONG GOALS	SIX-MONTH PLAN
1. School: Graduate from college	Do my homework every day Earn a 4.0 GPA this semester/quarter Visit one college campus with my parents/mentors
2. Home: Have a happy family	Spend more time with my family each day Help with household chores Write in my journal weekly
3. Work: Pursue a career I love	Visit two people at work to learn what they do Update my financial budget every week Read a good book cover to cover
4. Health: Live a healthy lifestyle	Exercise three times each week Stop eating so much sugar Find time to meditate/ponder daily
5. Service: Serve others daily	Volunteer at a local service organization at least once a month Make a new friend at school Offer to help friends with homework
6. Fun: Enjoy life!	Beat my high score on my favorite game Join a club at school Play my favorite sport/instrument/activity every week

CONVERSATION 3:
TIME MANAGEMENT

"Determine never to be idle. No person will have occasion to complain of the want of time who never loses any. It is wonderful how much can be done if we are always doing."

—*Thomas Jefferson*

LISTEN. We truly believe time management is one of the most important factors in achieving success. Every living person has the exact same amount of time. How we use it depends entirely on us.

The first thing we need to talk about is the importance of organizing your time by putting your schedule in writing. This can happen in a variety of ways, but the two most common are in a handwritten planner or an electronic calendaring system on your phone and computer. We suggest that you choose the latter because of the ability to sync across devices, set one-time and recurring appointments and alerts, and access various databases such as contacts or notes.

Even if you don't think so, your life is busy. We know that you have a morning routine (because you were so motivated by our last conversation), you have school with certain classes each day, you have homework, you have after-school activities, you have mealtimes, you have friends, and you have hobbies—to name a few things. You need to start putting all of this in a calendar so you are organized. For example, at the beginning of a new school year, you get a list of expectations and assignments/quizzes/exams called an outline or syllabus. Have you ever gone home with that syllabus and entered all the due dates into your calendar? Why not? You need to know when things are due so they don't sneak up on you. If your science teacher has a final project due in four months, then enter it into your calendar with a recurring monthly reminder. You can even go as far as scheduling time after school that says, "Work on science project." This way you are able to be at ease in class knowing that you have already taken the necessary steps to be prepared. Also, few of your teachers, if any at all, do not coordinate with each other; so you may have three exams in one week and not know about it until that week comes up because you didn't write them down. If you had organized your calendar in advance, then you would have expected the week coming up to be rough and would have prepared for it.

Having a robust and detailed calendar takes a lot of time, especially if this is new for you. Don't worry. Once you get into it, you will find planning to be quite enjoyable because you will see yourself becoming more productive. As your calendar fills up, knowing what areas of your life need improvement will be more apparent. One way to organize your calendar is by using different colors for different types of events, so that you can visually see the events separated. You can attach notes to the event and even set reminders. Also, you can invite and share events with friends and classmates. Use the amazing technology available to you. Channel it into becoming a productive student now and through high school.

Find a balance between all of your responsibilities and the things you want to do for fun. If there is a concert in a few months or a movie you pre-bought tickets for, then put it in your calendar. You will find yourself looking forward to these types of events, and as you get more familiar with your calendar, you will discover that you indeed have more time than you think. Perhaps the most pervasive problem students face today is the overuse of technology such as gaming and social media. There comes a time when you need to turn your technology off and focus on the important tasks at hand. Nothing will cause a student to fail more than this addictive distraction. If you are not capable of doing this on your own, parents/mentors should intervene.

Many will say that every minute of every day does not need to be planned. In fact, there is a saying from an anonymous author that goes, "Never trust a person who doesn't have time to read a good book." We believe in this concept. Of course we want to have time for good reading; nevertheless, having a detailed and documented calendar will allow you to foresee those times when you just need to relax. Spontaneous activities that bring us happiness can fit into a schedule—in fact, we've even got to the point of planning free time into our calendar! As you become more organized, you will have more control of your time.

The next thing we want to talk to you about is e-mail. You may already have an e-mail account or two that are set up with various online websites such as social media or online stores. If not, please ask your parents/mentors to help you obtain one. Make sure that your e-mail address is appropriate and easy to affiliate with your name. One time we sat in on the interview of a student whose e-mail address was "ihateschool@email.com." Needless to say, he did not go into the interview with the best initial reputation. If possible, use an e-mail address that has your first and last name so it appears professional.

Most of the communicating you will do in your academic life with teachers and classmates is going to be through e-mail and other electronic means. Always make sure your inbox is organized. For example, you can log-in to your e-mail and start going through every message. First and foremost, delete the junk. In fact, don't just delete it but make sure you don't receive it. Most companies who send you junk e-mail put an unsubscribe link in small print at the bottom of the e-mail. If they do not, your e-mail account has a setting to filter the e-mail so that you don't receive it again from that sender. Furthermore, use the e-mail account resources available to you such as folders and tags. You will be happy when you do these things, and you will feel the satisfaction of being organized.

Developing the habit of being a great time manager is tough. When you are sitting in a meeting and someone announces an upcoming activity, you need to train yourself to pull out your phone or tablet or computer and put in the activity right then and there. Don't wait, because you won't remember it later. You will also find that other people will start respecting you more because you will remember their activities and important dates, and you will be known as a person who shows up to events or at least apologizes in advance for not being available. Nothing is more annoying than someone who doesn't plan for or forgets an important event.

LEARN. Jill is a former classmate and friend of ours who understands what it means to manage time. For about four months, we were in the same classes as Jill, and we were able to witness firsthand and learn from her organizational techniques.

Over the summer before our classes even began, our teachers assigned heavy reading and writing assignments to bring to the first day of class. The accompanying assignments were not small. We're talking about 15 books and essays! On top of this, we averaged over 400 pages of weekly reading and over 10 pages of writing assignments throughout the semester. This was an intense scholarship program and truly forced us to manage our time. While many scholars experienced high levels of stress, Jill always remained calm, collected, and ahead of the class.

One specific day we remember sitting next to Jill. She had a sort of obsession, if you will, with anything Disney. Many of her school supplies were Disney-themed. Next to her Mickey Mouse calculator, Jill kept her planner, a collection of sticky notes, and various colored labels. This was a girl who definitely had a system that made sense to her, and really, that's all that mattered.

As the teacher started to assign the various homework projects, Jill went to work. Each class was color coded, and homework was highlighted and assigned a specific time, depending on the amount of homework given out. It is no wonder that Jill was prepared for every class with great comments and could summarize all of the pre-class reading because she scheduled sufficient time to complete the assignments. Learning became enjoyable for her, and her reputation in class was so stellar that when students didn't know an answer, they would say, "I don't know, ask Jill!"

Another one of Jill's impressive qualities was her dependability. She attended every class and social event and remembered special occasions as well. For example, she remembered our birthday, which we had only mentioned once in a casual conversation. She must have quickly put it into her phone and set a reminder. Now that was cool. These are the types of time-management skills that make a successful student and a reputable person.

REFLECT. Please take as much time as you need to ponder the following questions, and with the help of your parents/mentors, fill in your answers in the space provided.

What type of planning tools are you currently using?

none

Are there time management devices or methods that you are not utilizing?

all of them

If you had time to read any book right now, which one would you choose?

Dreamology

What kinds of responsibilities or events do you tend to miss often?

my chores

How could you better organize and manage your e-mail account?

Delete spam

What are the most important things in your life to make time for?

Family, Self care

Time Management

ACTION: In this section you will be taking time to thoroughly plan out an entire week. Think about everything you must accomplish and everything you want to accomplish. Refer to this calendar throughout your day and make decisions based on your plans. We encourage you to get in the habit of planning each week.

Please visit www.beatthemiddle.com/act to download this template.

	Monday	Tuesday	Wednesday	Thursday	Friday	Saturday	Sunday
6:00 AM							
6:30 AM							
7:00 AM							
7:30 AM							
8:00 AM							
8:30 AM							
9:00 AM							
9:30 AM							
10:00 AM							
10:30 AM							
11:00 AM							
11:30 AM							
12:00 PM							
12:30 PM							
1:00 PM							
1:30 PM							
2:00 PM							
2:30 PM							
3:00 PM							
3:30 PM							
4:00 PM							
4:30 PM							
5:00 PM							
5:30 PM							
6:00 PM							
6:30 PM							
7:00 PM							
7:30 PM							
8:00 PM							
8:30 PM							
9:00 PM							
9:30 PM							
10:00 PM							

Example on Back...

03

CONVERSATION

TIME MANAGEMENT EXAMPLE:

	Monday	Tuesday	Wednesday	Thursday	Friday	Saturday	Sunday
6:00 AM	Wake up & exercise	Wake up & exercise	Wake up & exercise	Wake up & exercise	Wake up & exercise		
6:30 AM	Shower & get ready	Shower & get ready	Shower & get ready	Shower & get ready	Shower & get ready		
7:00 AM	Personal time	Personal time	Personal time	Personal time	Personal time		
7:30 AM	School	School	School	School	School		
8:00 AM	Homework Due: Biology project, math assignment 1, and music hours sheet	Homework Due: English Essay draft and design for yearbook	Homework Due: Math assignment 2	Homework Due: Final introduction in English essay and solo competition is today in music		Mow Lawn & Clean Room	
8:30 AM							Church
9:00 AM							
9:30 AM						University Campus Tour	
10:00 AM							
10:30 AM							
11:00 AM							
11:30 AM							
12:00 PM							
12:30 PM							Nap Time!
1:00 PM							
1:30 PM							
2:00 PM							
2:30 PM							
3:00 PM	Tennis practice	Drama club	Tennis practice	Drama club	Tennis practice		
3:30 PM							
4:00 PM							
4:30 PM		Homework		Homework		Homework	Dinner at Grand- parents
5:00 PM							
5:30 PM	Family Dinner	Family Dinner	Family Dinner	Family Dinner	Family Dinner		
6:00 PM							
6:30 PM	Homework	Practice Piano	Homework	Watch TV			
7:00 PM			Hang Out with Friends		Volunteer at Pet Shelter	Go to Basketball Game with Friends	
7:30 PM							
8:00 PM	Family Activity	Watch TV		Church Activty			
8:30 PM							
9:00 PM							Write in Journal
9:30 PM							
10:00 PM	Read & Sleep	Read & Sleep	Read & Sleep	Read & Sleep	Read & Sleep	Read & Sleep	Read & Sleep

CONVERSATION 4:
GPA

"We are taught you must blame your father, your sisters, your brothers, the school, the teachers— but never blame yourself. It's never your fault. But it's always your fault, because if you wanted to change you're the one who has got to change."

—*Katharine Hepburn*

LISTEN. The uniqueness of this book is the fact that we are preparing you to think about college at an earlier age—before even beginning high school. One of the main reasons we are doing this is so you can start off on the right track with your grades. Colleges will start counting grades at the beginning of high school, which typically starts in ninth grade; nevertheless, earning good grades before ninth grade is crucial because you begin to form your study habits and routines.

Too often we see high school juniors and seniors who have poor grade point averages (GPA's), and there is nothing anybody can do about it. It's too late. You can't go back and change your grades as you are finishing high school, and grades are extremely important in college admissions. Many colleges in America are trying to get to a system where they can evaluate you on much more than grades. This is called holistic admissions, and we are advocates for this movement. This approach looks at grades, test scores, involvement, diversity, overcoming hardships, etc. However, most community and public colleges still have what is called an index score for their admissions process, which is a combination of your grades and test scores. The index score is calculated using a table like on the game Battleship. In Battleship you may say to your opponent "B5," and they go down to row "B" and over to column "5" to check and see if you have hit one of their ships. Well, in the case of a student who has a 3.8 GPA and a 28 ACT score, the college representative goes from a 4.0 GPA to 3.8 GPA and down from a 36 ACT to a 28 ACT, and the number found at the intersection is your index score. The higher your GPA and test score, the higher your index score. In most cases, everything from admissions to scholarship awards is based on index scores.

We often hear that grades aren't everything or some students are just naturally good at earning A's. Well, of course grades aren't everything. We hope that you have many goals in life beyond earning good grades, but in terms of going to college, your GPA is an accurate predictor of your future academic success. You must strive for good grades in addition to being well-rounded. As for those who "naturally get A's"—we don't buy it. Too often we have found that those who work the hardest earn the best grades. There are the occasional bright students who blow our minds, but even they started preparing sometime in their life. You can teach yourself to be this way with hard work and the right guidance. Fortunately, a high GPA does not always mean you are required to be the smartest student in class, only the hardest working.

Importantly, each of us has our own learning challenges, and for the more extensive cases, we would hope that your school and parents/mentors are advising you. Colleges have helpful resources as well and consider learning challenges in their application process; however, for the average student, grades and test scores are the major indicators considered in college admissions.

Learning is definitely the most important part of school. After high school your grades will get you into college, and your grades in college will keep you in college and will likely help you get a good job (especially when you are competing with many applicants— grades are an easy filter), but the day will come when you will be asked to show someone what you've learned. You may have received an A in history, but can you really explain the details of World War II? You may have a 4.0 GPA, but can you analyze a struggling company and find their problems? We recognize that learning is much more important than having a high GPA; but to get into the college of your choice and to land your dream job, you must place a heavy emphasis on earning good grades, which shouldn't be hard if you put in the time to learn the material you are given.

You can do certain things to get good grades. First, you have to complete and turn your assignments in on time. All of them! It doesn't matter if you think you won't learn anything from a particular assignment, you've got to have something to turn in. Teachers will work with you if you are consistently trying to learn in class and attempting every assignment. Some students feel they need a phone, tablet, or laptop in class to take notes, but they are deceiving themselves and stunting their learning. You may be surprised to know that at many universities students are only allowed paper and pencil in class to foster early preparation and a more engaging learning environment.

Second, if possible, make sure to research the right teachers for your learning style. Ask other students at your school about the teachers they've had. Do you like teachers who use a lot of group activities and visual presentations, or do you prefer a teacher who lectures while you take notes? We understand that in middle school and high school your options are limited. Sometimes there is only one teacher for a certain class, and you have no choice, but occasionally you can choose; make sure you've done your research.

Third, be sure to schedule time for homework each day. If you didn't already do this in your weekly calendar from Conversation 3, then go back and do it. Make sure you give yourself enough time. Maybe start with two hours each day, and if you finish early, great, but most days you will need that much time to do your assignments and read ahead for the next day. In fact, we've had some assignments that have taken more than two hours to complete; so be prepared each week to tailor your calendar to the needs of each class.

Taking easy classes may get you a high GPA, but you will regret this in the long run. The most competitive colleges look at your transcript and evaluate your GPA based on the courses you took; so don't be afraid to challenge yourself. You will learn more and, yes, it will be harder to maintain a high GPA, but believe in yourself and what you can do. Get help from family, friends, other students, and tutoring services. There is no reason why you can't have a difficult course load and earn good grades.

Be mindful that, in the future, you will have the opportunity to take college-level courses while in high school. These classes are great because you earn college credit without having to pay tuition. Remember the story of Bryce in Conversation 2? He had two years of college credits done while still in high school. Nevertheless, we also want to issue a word of caution here. We took several of these classes but nothing beyond our limits. Many people we knew overloaded on college credits while in high school but weren't the "Bryce's" of the world. They ended up sacrificing a high GPA that would have paid for their higher education through a scholarship. Make sure you know your limits.

Okay, so here is a semi-random question... do your parents/mentors trust you? Can you do many things that you want to do without always having to ask for their permission? It is natural for parents/mentors to question you, but as you enter high school, try to get straight A's for an entire year and see how their trust grows. It's remarkable how earning good grades will allow you more flexibility with your parents/mentors because they trust you.

Now, we have to warn you, it bothers us when elaborate rewards are either offered by parents/mentors or expected by students for earning good grades. While it can be very effective, you want to get good grades for the right reasons—learning, setting a good example, and preparing for college. The real reward will come in bigger and better ways than some sort of short-term prize. We promise!

The last thing we want to mention in this section is the importance of honesty. Nothing in life is worth compromising your reputation as an honest person, especially earning good grades. Cheating in school is wrong; however, we know it is tempting. As identical twins, we were tempted a few times to copy each other's answers or even switch clothes and take tests for each other! Nobody is free from having the temptation to cheat, and sometimes you can get away with it pretty easily. Nevertheless, don't be afraid to stand up for what is right. If you witness cheating, you have a responsibility to report it.

LEARN. Kelsey was a student in our same grade throughout middle school and high school. We were never part of the "popular" student group, but we had a small group of close friends, and Kelsey was one of them. Kelsey was quite popular in her own way. She was a cute girl who loved her family, church, school, and painting. She was well-rounded and had clear goals. Kelsey also had incredible grades. She got along well with our teachers and always put emphasis on getting homework done before doing anything else.

Many times we remember calling Kelsey to plan something with our friends, and she would say something like, "Well I won't be done with homework and dinner until after six thirty, so why don't we plan on seven?" What was even more impressive is that you could tell that Kelsey wasn't saying that because her parents told her to. She just understood that her parents would let her be with friends because they saw her first dedicate time to homework and family.

As Kelsey went through high school, she continued to get good grades, which enabled her to help others. She set a good example. As high school ended, Kelsey knew she would get into college. She applied to several institutions and was offered opportunities for admissions and scholarships at all of them. Her hard work literally paid off, and she continued to have a successful education and life.

Kelsey's story is extraordinary but you would never know it. She never had all the attention on her and she never wanted it. Kelsey just knew at an early age, even as early as seventh grade, that certain grades were needed to keep all her options open. Just because Kelsey's story sounds simple does not mean she didn't have obstacles. In fact, maintaining a high GPA demands many stressful nights trying to figure out a complicated math problem or finish a final paper or project. This doesn't even factor in the family struggles and friendship drama we all experience. Tears were shed, hope was lost, and Kelsey's parents/mentors needed to step in and help at times, but in the end, her determination and honest work ethic made Kelsey the successful person she is today.

REFLECT. Please take as much time as you need to ponder the following questions, and with the help of your parents/mentors, fill in your answers in the space provided.

What would stand in your way of averaging higher than a 3.8 GPA?

Lack of motivation

What times and locations are best for you to do homework?

At night in my bed

What types of classes are you most interested in taking?

English and performing classes

Do you prefer certain teaching styles over others?

I prefer flash cards and hands on activities

How would having more trust from your parents/mentors change your life?

I would be happier

What are the most tempting ways to cheat for you, and how can you overcome these temptations?

_____ none _____

_____

CONVERSATION

GPA

ACTION:

Your GPA is crucial to academic success, so it is important that you routinely track it. Every three months you should write down your current GPA and your cumulative GPA (average of all GPAs). Remember that, for better or worse, your cumulative GPA is tracked the entire time you are in high school (9th – 12th grade) and is the GPA that colleges will evaluate you on.

Please visit www.beatthemiddle.com/act to download this template.

GPA TRACKER

	July–Sept		Oct–Dec		Jan–Mar		Apr–Jun	
	Current	Cumulative	Current	Cumulative	Current	Cumulative	Current	Cumulative
7TH GRADE								
8TH GRADE								
9TH GRADE								
10TH GRADE								
11TH GRADE								
12TH GRADE								

GPA EXAMPLE:

GPA TRACKER

	July–Sept		Oct–Dec		Jan–Mar		Apr–Jun	
	Current	Cumulative	Current	Cumulative	Current	Cumulative	Current	Cumulative
7TH GRADE	4.0	4.0	3.9	3.95	4.0	3.967	4.0	3.975
8TH GRADE	4.0	3.98	4.0	3.983	3.9	3.971	3.8	3.95
9TH GRADE	4.0	3.955						
10TH GRADE								
11TH GRADE								
12TH GRADE								

CONVERSATION 5:

COLLEGE ENTRANCE EXAMS

"The price of success is hard work, dedication to the job at hand, and the determination that whether we win or lose, we have applied the best of ourselves to the task at hand."

—*Vince Lombardi*

LISTEN. Have you heard the saying, "There are two sides to every story"? Well, we have found this is the case with college entrance exams. Most students believe they are truly poor test takers. This belief occurs because we, as humans, get nervous and anxious when we are put under pressure to recite things from memory. Tests can be misleading because some people really know the information, but their nerves get the best of them. The other side of the story is that tests are an excellent way to demonstrate knowledge. With the right amount of preparation and studying, you can be a good test taker. The GPA of a student may show ability to do homework and work hard over time, but a test really shows what an individual knows at one moment in time. We could go back and forth about this issue, but the fact of the matter is— you need to know how to test well because it not only affects your GPA, but it also affects the types of schools you can attend and how much scholarship money will be available to you.

There are two main college entrance exams. The first is the ACT (www.act.org) and the second is the SAT (www.sat.org). Colleges do not care which one you take because they are comparable in content and level of difficulty. Typically where you live will determine which test is available for you to take. Each test is structured to measure your knowledge in subjects such as English, reading, writing, mathematics, science, etc. If you want to learn more about the details of these exams, we encourage you to visit their websites and seek help from your parents/mentors.

The biggest mistake you can make with the ACT or SAT is not taking it early enough. Some states are now requiring all high school students to take the test during their junior year in high school. This is awesome, but why was it necessary to make it mandatory?

Because not enough students were preparing for and taking the exam early! Don't be that student. In our opinion, you should plan now to test at least three times BEFORE your senior year of high school. Practice makes perfect. If you want to learn how to sing, then you don't sing the song for the first time on the night of a performance, right? Taking a test is a talent that must be practiced.

Preparing for the ACT/SAT includes scheduling time to study and register for the test in advance to give yourself a deadline. Many wonderful study aids are available to help you. Your school will have resources you can borrow for free. Use them! Free online resources are available to you as well, and your parents/mentors can help you access these through the websites provided above. The fact of the matter is, you have access to practice tests and questions starting now. Scheduling time to study for the ACT/SAT is as important as your GPA; so when you have a night with no homework scheduled, use that time to study for the exam. Chances are the studying will also help you with your classes. In fact, if you are strategic, you can coordinate topics on the exam with what you are learning in class. For example, if you are in a geometry class learning about finding the area of various shapes, then you can bet this is in the mathematics section of the ACT/SAT.

As mentioned earlier, be sure to give yourself a deadline for taking practice and actual ACT/SAT exams. You can go online and see all the dates for when the exam will be administered. Pick one as a deadline, register for it, and put it on your calendar. Again, you can always take it more than once. In fact, most colleges will allow you to submit up to 12 different college entrance exams. Set a goal of taking the tests several times, and be sure your goal also includes setting a desired score that is tough but realistic for your abilities. We believe that scoring higher on college entrance exams is definitely the most underutilized way to pay for school. Many scholarships are out there waiting for you.

LEARN. Okay so this is Blake writing now because I want to use Bo's experience in this part of the book because of what he did with the ACT exam.

Bo and I both knew we wanted to go to Utah State University (USU). It was far enough from home for us to be independent, yet close enough to drive home if we needed to. We both love tennis and were offered the opportunity to play for the USU team. This was an amazing experience, but it did not come with enough funding to cover four years' worth of tuition. In order to pay for our schooling, we researched other scholarships and found an on-campus leadership program that fit our talents and paid full tuition; however, Bo did not quite have the ACT score to apply for this scholarship.

I will never forget what Bo did. He was so determined to get his education paid for that he locked himself away and studied for weeks at a time. He registered for every ACT exam available that year, and in addition, took the ACT a few more times on Utah State's campus because it was offered to prospective students with the condition that the score could only be used at USU, which was fine for Bo. In the end, Bo took the ACT nine times! He finally reached his goal, and the scholarship covered tuition and fees for up to four years. Our gratitude for such scholarship programs cannot be described in words because it was our path to a higher education. Maybe you can relate. If so, follow Bo's example and get the score you need.

FLECT. Please take as much time as you need to ponder the lowing questions, and with the help of your parents/mentors, fill in your answers in the space provided.

How important is it for you personally to learn more about the ACT/SAT?

_____

_____

When can you make regular time to study for the ACT/SAT?

_____

_____

How will your parents/mentors help you study for the ACT/SAT?

_____

_____

What would stand in your way of scoring above 90 percent?

_____

_____

What kind of score would you need to get a scholarship at the colleges near your home?

_____

_____

How can you overcome your nervousness on exams?

_____

_____

College Entrance Exams

ACTION:

Both the ACT and SAT exam require practice, like playing an instrument or sport. The chart below allows you to track when you take practice exams and real exams. Our suggestion is that you take the real exam at least three times before your senior year of high school and take at least three practice exams before each real exam. If you are not happy with your score by the time you start your senior year, then you will want to take the exam as many times as you need to until you are satisfied.

Please visit www.beatthemiddle.com/act to download this template.

COLLEGE ENTRANCE EXAMS

	Practice 1		Practice 2		Practice 3		Take Actual Test	
	Date	Score	Date	Score	Date	Score	Date	Score
9TH GRADE								
10TH GRADE								
11TH GRADE								
12TH GRADE								

COLLEGE ENTRANCE EXAMS EXAMPLE:

ACT EXAM SCORES

	Practice 1		Practice 2		Practice 3		Take Actual Test	
	Date	Score	Date	Score	Date	Score	Date	Score
9TH GRADE	06/15	17	09/02	20	02/22	19	03/05	19
10TH GRADE	07/02	21	10/25	23	04/09	23	04/10	23
11TH GRADE	06/20	23	09/15	24	03/01	25	03/03	26
12TH GRADE	06/29	25	09/24	25	03/08	27	03/09	29

CONVERSATION 6:

INTERNSHIPS AND WORK EXPERIENCE

"The only source of knowledge is experience."

—*Albert Einstein*

LISTEN. We are sure that you hope to be employed one day and not just in a job but in a career you enjoy, right? Well, the pathway to get there has certainly been laid out so far, but this conversation is a very important piece of the puzzle. To land a great career, you must have previous experience in jobs and internships. There are a couple of differences between working at a job and working as an intern. A job is something you are paid to do, and usually you are expected to continually do that job unless you quit or are fired. On the other hand, an internship is a job-like experience that is set up for a specific amount of time, such as three months, six months, or whatever is agreed upon. An internship can be paid or unpaid depending on the arrangement.

Working a job and completing internships as a student is becoming more and more common. Although some people may see this as a bad thing because you should be studying, we are of the opinion you can do both. You should seek these types of experiences because they offer several important benefits, including the valuable experience you gain by being around professionals, the work ethic you learn, and the additional income you will earn.

The most valuable lesson we can help you understand during this conversation is the idea that volunteering for an unpaid internship can be one of the most strategic and rewarding things you ever do. First, you have to figure out what you like to do and what you are good at. There are experiences out there that will be much better for your résumé if you volunteer. Do not limit yourself by only targeting paid opportunities. For example, let's say you want to be a graphic designer someday, but you don't have the credentials to land a job as a designer yet because you are still learning. You may easily be able to go down the street to every store or company in your neighborhood and get a job doing something else, but what if you walked into the best design firm in your town and volunteered for their team? Almost every time we've tried this, it has worked because there is no downside—the company gets free help, and you will gain career-specific experience. Also, you will develop relationships that will lead to future references and letters of recommendation for jobs and college admissions. It's a win-win situation.

The best first step in gaining internship and work experience is an in-person meeting. Make sure you set up an appointment and go in looking like a professional with a ready résumé and a positive attitude. Just because you are young and willing to volunteer your time doesn't mean you shouldn't be impressive, because you will be working on important projects, and many times an unpaid internship, if done well, can turn into a paid internship or even a job. If an in-person meeting is not going to work out because of the person's schedule, then writing a professional e-mail is very appropriate. Keep it short and to the point. Attach your résumé and compliment the company's successes—after all, you are impressed with them; if you weren't, you wouldn't want to work there, right?

Doing your research allows you to talk intelligently about the company. Your interest in their work can result in their interest in you. Be genuine in your request, and discuss ways you will contribute to the company's successes. Request a follow-up phone conversation or in-person meeting to discuss the opportunity further. This is the process we have used in most of the experiences on our résumés. It works well.

Many times we had a volunteer internship experience on top of a regular job that provided some money. We were tennis instructors, basketball referees, lifeguards, waiters, etc. This may be the case for you too, and if it is, then do not worry—it can be done. All of these jobs teach you something. We learned to value working with kids, teaching others new skills, and serving people—qualities that come in handy each day of our lives. Remember, as we mentioned earlier in the book, make sure you are documenting all of these experiences, both the internships and the paid jobs that you have. If internships and work experiences start to take away from your academic success, then it's time to scale back. Your main focus should be school. The experiences are great and necessary but not to the point of sacrificing your grades.

Make sure that you are always using the services available to you when it comes to looking for internship and work experiences. Family and friends are good places to start, and in addition, there are many services at your school and in the community that connect people, even young people, with great opportunities.

Be aware of opportunities you can provide for others. You may have an uncle who runs a company that you have no interest in, but maybe your friends do, or someone you know who may be looking for a job could benefit from your telling them about your uncle. You never know how you can change another person's life through connecting them to internship and work experiences.

Looking and acting professionally in all settings is important. Many companies will look you up online; if you haven't ever looked yourself up online, then we suggest doing it. See what you can find out about yourself as if you were the one doing the hiring. Are there any unprofessional pictures that you find online? How about the way you write and express yourself to others? When you apply for jobs, you are basically putting yourself out there to be noticed, and people will see your name and look you up, which is easy to do these days. They will also ask others about you, so it is very important to be a kind person who remains professional in the way you present yourself both online and in person.

LEARN. Sam is our cousin, and ever since we can remember, even before middle school, he would come up with ideas to make extra money. It all started out with our boyhood club, BB&S (Bo, Blake, and Sam). Whether it was routine yard work or washing someone's boat, we did all kinds of jobs. This work ethic stuck with Sam throughout middle school and high school. He worked many jobs to support himself such as busing tables, making sandwiches, and watching children at a daycare. He also worked at two car washes and a hearing aid company.

As for an internship, Sam was in love with the idea of working for a professional sports team, specifically the Utah Jazz basketball team. Sam has been a Jazz fan for his entire life, and one day he finally realized the opportunity had come to work with the team. Sam's family had just moved into a new neighborhood where a man in a house down the street worked with the Jazz. Sam was professional and upfront about his desire to work with the team and even volunteered to shadow his neighbor at work. Their relationship grew into a friendship, and Sam had many meaningful experiences with the team and the general management of the organization.

After graduating from high school, Sam received many letters of recommendation for future jobs and internships that were written by the individuals he worked with. Sam decided to pursue higher education and is currently working on a bachelor's degree in order to further his career. In addition to studying, Sam is working and interning part-time. We have no doubt that upon graduation, Sam will be able to take his diploma, coupled with his vast amount of internship and work experience, and start a wonderful career.

REFLECT. Please take as much time as you need to ponder the following questions, and with the help of your parents/mentors, fill in your answers in the space provided.

What does the ideal career look like to you?

Flexible and fun

What internship and work experiences do you want to have?

working with teachers and waiters

Do you have family, friends, and/or neighbors who can help you get a job or an internship?

my grandma

Do you know someone who could help others with a job or internship?

_no_

Does any of your online information make you uncomfortable?

no

How many hours each week would you be able to work and/or volunteer?

about 24-30

CONVERSATION

06

**BEAT
THE
MIDDLE**

Internships and Work Experience

ACTION:

One of the techniques we discussed in Conversation 2 – Planning and Preparation is the idea that you are always aware of what is on your current résumé and what should be on your future résumé. As you have various internship and work experiences, you should be writing them down on a template such as the one we're providing. We've split the template into sections to get you thinking about everything you will need on a good résumé. This is an evolving document that should constantly be updated.

Please visit www.beatthemiddle.com/act to download this template.

RESUME TEMPLATE

Education	
Professional Experience	
Leadership & Service	
Honor & Awards	
Professional Organizations	
References	

Example on Back…

© 2014 Blake & Bo Nemelka

CONVERSATION

INTERNSHIP & WORK EXPERIENCE EXAMPLE:

RESUME TEMPLATE

Education	*Riverton High School* *Riverton, Utah* *3.9 GPA*
Professional Experience	*Helped my uncle in the summers teaching tennis lessons* *Worked for the family business on some weekends – 2010 to 2014* *Interned with neighbor, Swendy, at her daycare from June to* *December, 2013*
Leadership & Service	*Captain of tennis team – 9th grade* *Volunteer at pet shelter – once a week* *Church group service*
Honor & Awards	*Most improved player for tennis* *2nd place in piano recital*
Professional Organizations	*National Honor Society – >3.75 GPA during 7th through 9th grade*
References	*Swendy, church leaders, English teacher...*

Example on Back...

CONVERSATION 7:

EXTRA- AND CO-CURRICULAR ACTIVITIES

"When I was a teenager, I began to settle into school because I'd discovered the extracurricular activities that interested me: music and theater."

—*Morgan Freeman*

LISTEN. When we were in middle school, there was a definite emphasis on getting involved in extracurricular activities; however, there was no mention of co-curricular activities. So what is the difference between the two?

Not too long ago, we were invited to team up with a college professor of ours at Utah State and research student activities. We concluded that extracurricular activities are done outside your study area because of enjoyment and a desire to be involved. Maybe you want to study business, but you like to play tennis and sing, so you try out for the tennis team and city choir group. A co-curricular activity is one that is directly related to an academic interest—it is part of what you like to study. For example, if you are studying art and you join the art club, that would be a co-curricular activity.

As you prepare for the future, being involved and well-rounded in your extra- and co-curricular activities is important. In our opinion, extra- and co-curricular activities are where you gain valuable experience in several key areas of happiness, including your social life, spirituality, and physical health. Try to branch out enough to include these areas in your daily and weekly routines. Be sure you are connecting with others (your future friends and study partners), finding time for yourself, meditating, and staying fit. Participation in various types of clubs, hobbies, and other activities sets you apart and defines your uniqueness. Every student will have a GPA, but not every student joins a chess club.

Having a robust résumé that includes a variety extra- and co-curricular involvement is important because colleges and employers want to see that you have many different background experiences; however, be sure you are having fun. It is possible to be having fun and building your résumé at the same time. Don't look for a certain club or event just because you think it will look good on your résumé. This is the wrong type of motivation. Go out and look for things that interest you and that you sincerely want to learn more about. This way you are still building your experiences, but the fact that you are enjoying yourself will drive you to learn even more and benefit from the time you are putting into it. Also, do not just sign up for a lot of activities without dedicating quality time to them. It's easy to tell when a student has just signed up for every club on the planet and maybe attends a couple meetings each year versus the student who sticks to one or two clubs and is actively involved in them on a weekly, if not daily, basis.

Furthermore, being an active participant will result in various leadership opportunities. Most clubs or sports are in need of good leaders who will help others engage in the activity as well. Look for those opportunities, and if they don't exist, then make them happen yourself. Become a leader in what you enjoy doing, and if there is no official club, then become the founder.

If you haven't been able to tell yet, we are advocates for staying engaged in life-improving activities. This can be busy and overwhelming, but if you remember what we talked about in Conversation 3 regarding time management, then you will be just fine. Also, if you are engaged in fun, productive activities, then why not stay busy, right? What you want to avoid is being busy with something that is unproductive, such as playing video games, watching television/movies, and messing around with inappropriate Internet and social media websites. Don't get us wrong—we have fun too! Some of our favorite "unproductive" things in middle school were movie marathons and playing Nintendo 64. Have you ever spent an entire afternoon/evening watching every episode in a TV series or maybe trying to pass levels in a video game? Maybe you spend too much time worrying about your social media. Whatever the case may be, you know what tempts you and what needs to be controlled. You can also have fun participating in productive activities. For example, we enjoyed playing tennis together, spending time with friends, and reading popular books.

Having defined goals is the first step to being productive because you will be able to keep your focus while still having fun along the way. Also, if you are mindful of the way you manage your extra- and co-curricular involvement, then you may just get all or part of your college paid for through a scholarship program that values skills like leadership and qualities that come from highly involved individuals.

LEARN. During our freshmen year of college, we had the opportunity to interact with many students who had been very involved in extra- and co-curricular activities throughout middle school and high school. One of those students, and a dear friend of ours, is named Brent. Anybody who knew Brent in college, and many did, knew that he was a loyal friend and a fantastic student leader.

Throughout middle school and high school Brent was involved in student government, event planning, marketing clubs, and several other personal hobbies. He had many friends and a busy social schedule to juggle. These experiences helped Brent apply for and receive a prestigious college scholarship that was meant for highly social and involved students. Basically Brent paid for his entire bachelor's degree doing what he already enjoyed doing—being proactively involved in school activities and events while encouraging others to do the same.

We enjoyed watching Brent throughout college because his drive and passion for marketing, web design, and sales grew in the classroom, and his social and leadership skills were developed outside of class through his scholarship and other student-involvement groups.

The best part about Brent is that his involvement did not stop once his schooling was paid for. He enjoys being involved so much that the art of staying busy and actively engaged has continued on throughout college and even into his career, making him a respected and successful professional who is fun to be around. Even to this day, Brent looks for opportunities to grow and develop himself in his career. The habits that were formed at an early age have only gained strength over the years and made Brent into one of the most successful and high-spirited people we know.

REFLECT. Please take as much time as you need to ponder the following questions, and with the help of your parents/mentors, fill in your answers in the space provided.

What do you like to do for fun?

_____

_____

What types of extracurricular activities interest you?

_____

_____

What types of co-curricular activities interest you?

_____

_____

Do you have an idea about what you want to study in college and what you want your career to be one day?

_____

_____

What are the time-wasting activities that most tempt you, and what are you going to do about it?

_____

_____

What area of your life is in most need of more extra- and co-curricular involvement?

_____

_____

CONVERSATION

Extra- and Co-Curricular Activities

ACTION:

The template provided in this section requires you to fill out two extracurricular activities and two co-curricular activities that describe your interests. These activities can include clubs, hobbies, professional organizations, etc. Take some time to fill in the activities you are currently involved in and/or would like to be involved in. Write a short description of the activity, the name and contact information of the person in charge, and a list of meeting times to put into your weekly calendar.

Please visit www.beatthemiddle.com/act to download this template.

EXTRACURRICULAR ACTIVITIES

	Description	Name/Contact	Meeting Times
Activity #1			
Activity #2			

CO-CURRICULAR ACTIVITIES

	Description	Name/Contact	Meeting Times
Activity #1			
Activity #2			

Example on Back…

BEAT
THE
MIDDLE

EXTRA- AND CO-CURRICULAR ACTIVITIES EXAMPLE:

EXTRACURRICULAR ACTIVITIES

	Description	Name/Contact	Meeting Times
Activity #1 Tennis	Member of School Tennis Team	Coach Matthews Cell Phone: (xxx) xxx –xxxx	Monday's, Wednesday's, and Friday's from 3 – 5 PM
Activity #2 Piano	Take piano Lessons each week	Lori Cell Phone: (xxx) xxx –xxxx	Tuesday's at 6:30 PM

CO-CURRICULAR ACTIVITIES

	Description	Name/Contact	Meeting Times
Activity #1 Drama Club	Practicing to become an actress	Mr. Johnson mjohnson@email.edu	Tuesday's and Thursday's from 3 –4 PM
Activity #2 National Honor Society	Receive support in hard classes	Mrs. Kinzer skinzer@email.edu	Anytime during school or by appointment

CONVERSATION 8:

SERVICE

"Life's most persistent and urgent question is,
'What are you doing for others?'"

—Dr. Martin Luther King, Jr.

LISTEN. Upon reflection of our own experiences, we noticed that service played a major part in two ways. First, service was what others were doing for us as parents/mentors. Second, service is the key component to understanding true leadership and thus is an important part of what colleges and universities want to see in your background. Allow us to talk about both of these points further.

There is a concept in the universe that is known as collective thinking or karma or prayer. Whatever you may call it, there is power in "thinking happy thoughts" and "what goes around comes around" and "whatsoever ye shall ask...shall be given unto you." We are firm believers that you must recognize the service others are doing on your behalf and give them the appropriate gratitude and, at the same time, look for ways to serve those around you. Use the talents you have and look for ways to help others.

One of our professors in college and perhaps one of the most influential mentors in our lives is named Lynne. In one of Lynne's classes, we participated in an activity where we drafted a Personal Mission Statement. This type of statement is meant to be one sentence that defines your life's mission. In order to lead this discussion, Lynne started out with a question about the true meaning of leadership. Many students gave the obvious and true qualities of a leader—they are motivating, accomplished, driven, etc., but the conversation soon turned to service as a defining component of leadership. When Lynne shared his Personal Mission Statement, we felt its power. It was sincere, direct, and selfless. Lynne's statement read something like this, "I will live my life helping others recognize their full potential." What a statement of service and leadership! If you can understand this concept now at such a young age, then you will truly live an accomplished life.

Service towards others is important, and the types of service discussed so far are the most important. Nevertheless, you will need to seek various types of organized service opportunities to highlight on your résumé. At first we thought we just needed to list things that related to service, no matter our involvement. For example, our father received a heart transplant, and, as a result, was used in various marketing campaigns in Utah, especially because at that time Miss Utah was also promoting organ donation. We were able to attend a few events and even speak once so . . . throw it on the résumé and put it on college applications right? Well, yes, but be honest about what it was that you did. There is a big difference between saying that you helped once at an event and saying that you are a public speaker for the promotion of organ donation. If there is a cause that you want to support, such as organ donation in this example, then go out and get involved. Become the leader at your school with campaigns and fundraisers.

Having a sincere desire to serve a certain type of person, group, or cause is the ultimate need for real service. Just like with extra- and co-curricular activities, have fun doing it. Service will bring about the most enjoyable experiences life has to offer you, and an important side benefit is you are improving your résumé. College admissions representatives understand the meaning of true service. Time commitment and a passion to help will shine on your résumé, so make sure to have your focus in those areas rather than just a few events that you helped with one time. If you need help finding and joining organized service opportunities, ask your parents/mentors to guide you. You will be surprised at the infinite number of opportunities available to you at your school, in your community, and even on national and international levels.

LEARN. We want to tell you about David, our relative. He is a doctor whose life has been a pathway of service. When David was in middle school and high school, he was very kind and was the first to help a friend, a family member, or anybody in need. He was a Boy Scout and a young man of faith who attended regular church meetings and activities.

At the age of nineteen, David decided to take a break from his regular life of family and school to serve as a volunteer for two years. He spent these years in the Philippines helping others through spiritual messages, manual labor, and daily acts of service. As a volunteer, he did not have a cell phone or access to the Internet or even television.

When David returned from the Philippines, he decided to continue his education and prepare for medical school. He desired to attend a military medical school sponsored by the United States Air Force. David studied very hard to become a doctor of emergency medicine while also serving as a Captain in the Air Force and raising a family.

David is truly a great example who serves others as a volunteer, a member of the military, a doctor, and a family man. Each day he is saving lives one at a time. David lives a happy life because of the service he gives. Can you imagine what our world would be like if every one of us followed in David's footsteps? David was very smart in the way he set his goals—using the benefits of serving in the military to put himself through school. Do not underestimate the power and blessings that will come into your life when you put the needs of others before your own.

REFLECT. Please take as much time as you need to ponder the following questions, and with the help of your parents/mentors, fill in your answers in the space provided.

What does service mean to you?

_____

_____

Are there certain people and/or groups that you would like to serve?

_____

_____

How has serving others helped you so far in your life?

_____

_____

What types of activities are taking you away from being able to serve others?

_____

_____

What clubs or organizations would you want to join or start that revolve around service?

_____

_____

What resources are available to you in seeking service opportunities?

_____

_____

08

CONVERSATION

Service

ACTION:

Now is the time for you to write your own personal mission statement. Put serious thought into what you write. We encourage you to put this in a place where you can read it daily and reflect upon the words you've written.

Please visit www.beatthemiddle.com/act to download this template.

MY PERSONAL MISSION STATEMENT

Please write down your own personal mission statement and keep it in a place where you can read it each day.

SERVICE EXAMPLE:

MY PERSONAL MISSION STATEMENT

Please write down your own personal mission statement and keep it in a place where you can read it each day.

Each day I will live my life in a way that inspires others to achieve their full potential.

CONVERSATION 9:

MONEY MANAGEMENT AND SCHOLARSHIPS

"My mom played tennis for, like, six hours a day and went to college on a tennis scholarship, because that was the way she could go to school. So they [my parents] instilled in me the idea that you have to work hard for the things you want in life and never complain."

—*Dakota Fanning*

LISTEN. If we could help you understand only two princip[l] of money management, they would be, first, do not spend moꞁe money than you make, and second, be sure to set aside money for savings. As we discussed earlier in the book, you should seek opportunities to be a volunteer intern; however, you are more than likely going to need a job or other means of making some money. Unfortunately, this is how it goes for many families. Our guess would be that your parents/mentors do not have extra money to throw your way, and even if they did, this shouldn't happen because they should want you to earn it. Even if you are struggling financially, you can find ways to break out of this through hard work and wise money management. So, however you dedicate your time to earning money, it is important that your time is managed well and that you plan for your future.

Whatever educational path you decide to pursue after high school (college, trade school, certificate programs, etc.) will cost money . . . a lot of money. As you already may know, you have three options for paying for school: scholarships, cash, and/or loans. One of the main purposes of this book is to have the necessary conversations with you at a young enough age so that a scholarship is one of your realistic goals. Students with high GPA's, good test scores, a wealth of extra- and co-curricular activities, and internship and work experiences will get paid to go to school rather than pay for school. Colleges nearly fight each other for the top applicants, and this can and should be you. You need to remember while one college may not give you a scholarship, another might. Be smart in considering your options as you discuss them with your parents/mentors.

Everybody has an opinion about student loans, so the best we can do is simply share our opinion, which is—they are worth it

. . . to an extent. You must first exhaust several avenues before turning to loans. Those avenues are scholarships, family support, working, and grants. If your family is not in a position to help you, you do not have enough scholarship money to cover all the costs (tuition, fees, living expenses, etc.), you aren't able to work enough hours to cover the costs, or you don't qualify for grant money, then of course you should get a loan. Your education, if completed carefully, will no doubt allow you to get a good job and be able to pay back the loans.

In addition, you need to decide what amount is worth paying for a college education. This is dependent on several factors including, but not limited to, prestige of the school, location, quality of the education, and cost of living. If you have worked hard enough to the point of getting into a prestigious university, then having a manageable loan would be worth the investment. That's pretty obvious, right? You may feel under qualified right now, but the reason we are talking to you about this now is so you are aware of your potential early enough to reach it.

Both of us have proven this theory in our own lives. We decided to take community college classes and later attend a public state university to complete our bachelor's degrees because financially it made sense. However, the time came when we knew we had the potential, just like you, to think about and even attend prestigious academic programs. Now, you must know if you are going for this type of goal because you want the recognition, then you have missed our point. The point is for you to be able to push yourself and be rewarded for your hard work. If you take middle school and high school seriously and come out with the credentials we've talked about, then you, too, will have more opportunities, and that is something you should never be ashamed to pursue!

One last thing we want to mention is the need for you to sacrifice at times. We have been inspired by examples around us. When other people had laptops, many of our friends used the library computers. When other people had their own car, many used public transportation. Eat your lunch at the cafeteria or at home rather than going out to eat all the time. These are the simple, daily sacrifices that will go a long way—not just for your wallet but also for the type of person you will become.

LEARN. Brady and Tina are the examples that come to mind when thinking about wise money management. Having met in middle school theatre class, they became an inseparable couple with specific goals and many dreams of one day being a family and continuing all the hobbies they enjoy together. To this day Brady and Tina have more interests and are more involved than anyone we know. They love the outdoors, cooking, woodworking, theater productions, beekeeping, gardening, taking care of dogs, etc. The list goes on, but the point is that at a young age, Brady and Tina recognized that they needed to make smart decisions and budget their money well.

After finishing high school with good grades, Brady decided to enroll at the local four-year university as a finance and economics major. Brady worked night shifts at a local factory while interning for the company's finance department as well. Tina became the youngest manager of a local, popular candy store. Upon graduating, Brady was hired full-time in the finance department of the company he was working for and later moved to another company to work in a senior-level position. With two incomes Brady and Tina decided to create and follow a specific financial plan which involved setting aside money each month in various envelopes—limiting themselves to certain amounts of money for categories such as food, gas, entertainment, etc. Savings and charitable church donations were always first on their list of expenses, and then each month's fixed expenses were taken care of. They now own a beautiful home and are easily able to support any hobby they desire to pursue. Their "envelope budget" worked!

Brady and Tina are ideal examples of how normal students in middle school and high school can work hard and be smart in assuring their future ability to have a stable income and comfortable lifestyle. There is no secret to this type of success other than not spending more than you make and saving a portion of your money. Each of the conversations we have discussed build upon one another as can be seen in this example. In order for Brady and Tina to live the type of lives they do, you better believe they have been meticulously organized and focused on things like their grades and test scores. They interned and worked to get through school. They are two of many examples we know who represent academic and financial success—meaning they set their goals early and achieved them. While your goals may be slightly different than Brady and Tina's, the principles to achieve them remain the same.

REFLECT. Please take as much time as you need to ponder the following questions, and with the help of your parents/mentors, fill in your answers in the space provided.

How important is money to you?

_____

_____

Are you currently living below your means and saving?

_____

_____

What type of educational experience is worth a financial investment?

_____

_____

Who do you look up to in terms of financial success?

_____

_____

What type of lifestyle do you envision being happy with one day, and how much will it cost?

_____

_____

What hobbies do you enjoy, and what hobbies will you continue to enjoy as you age?

_____

_____

09

BEAT
THE
MIDDLE

Money Management and Scholarships

ACTION:

Routinely tracking the money you earn (income) and the money you spend (expenses) will allow you to better evaluate your current and future financial situation. Developing the habit of managing your finances is possible at your age and will provide you financial benefits in years to come.

Please visit www.beatthemiddle.com/act to download this template.

PERSONAL MONTHLY INCOME STATEMENT

Income		Expenses	
Amount	Description	Amount	Description
Total:		Total:	

MONEY MANAGEMENT AND SCHOLARSHIPS EXAMPLE:

PERSONAL MONTHLY INCOME STATEMENT

Income		Expenses	
Amount	Description	Amount	Description
$40.00	Allowance	$2.25	Snack
$10.00	Tennis Lesson	$8.00	Movie
$5.00	Spare Change	$5.25	Fast Food
$60.00	Presents	$35.96	New Music
		$63.54	Savings
Total: $115.00		Total: $115.00	

CONVERSATION 10:
THE APPLICATION PROCESS

"If you dare nothing, then when the day is over, nothing is all you will have gained."

—*Neil Gaiman*

LISTEN. Applying for anything can be an intimidating process, but you can follow certain principles no matter what you apply for. For the purposes of this book and conversation, we will use the example of applying for admission at a college or university. The college application process seems scary, but when you know the things we are going to teach you about, then it really is not that bad. It's mostly about timing and being honest.

First things first: start early. Heck, start now! Why not invite your family/friends and start going on campus tours of the colleges and universities near you? Once you cover those, then you can set goals to visit other schools of interest inside and outside of your state. How else will you know if they are a good fit for you? Also, a recurring theme throughout this conversation and section of the book is the importance of showing up in person versus just submitting an application online. Putting a name with a face and making a first impression is very powerful and, when done correctly, gives you an advantage.

Okay, so narrowing down your options by starting early is great. When the time comes for actually applying in your senior year of high school, you will know where to apply. In terms of submitting your application, you must be aware of the various deadlines a college has. There will be some for "early" applications, "priority" applications, "regular" applications, and "late" applications—to name a few. These deadlines don't even include applying for federal financial aid, and they may or may not include scholarships. The point is, know your deadlines! One of the biggest mistakes high school seniors make is thinking they have the whole year to apply to college. Most colleges offer their admissions application at the beginning of your senior year, and their scholarship deadlines keep moving up earlier and earlier, some even as early as November of the year before you graduate from high school. Now that you know this, do your research and plan accordingly.

A great phrase to keep in mind is, "It never hurts to apply." Instead of applying to one or two schools, why not apply to five or six? In most cases, the same information will be required, and even the essays (if required) are similar. The extra time and application fee money that you spend is worth having a few more options. Applications do not require any sort of commitment, so allow yourself the opportunity to choose from a good pool of schools.

Now that you understand the timing and expectations of the application process, we need to talk about the content of your application. Another key phrase to remember is "Honesty is the best policy." While it is an old, cliché phrase, honesty truly is the best policy when filling out applications. Admissions selection committees can see right through someone who is exaggerating information or lying. Our whole point in having these conversations with you now, at an early age, is to prepare you to know what selection committees look for and to encourage you to honestly strive for those qualities. They look for good grades, solid test scores, extra- and co-curricular involvement, and those who give back to others and their community through service. They look for someone with goals who knows what it means to lead others—all of which we have discussed in this book; so be honest in your application, and show what you've done to stand out. If you do all of these things, you will certainly be unique, because the majority of students applying do not have all of these points to boast about. Also, you may have diverse experiences based on the way you were raised or because of traits you were born with. Tell them about those experiences. You have nothing to lose when you are honest with yourself and on your application.

Last, it never hurts to get to know people and ask for recommendations from those you already know. Every now and then you'll associate with the kind person who was "paying attention" and offers to write a letter or make a call on your behalf without being asked. Although that is the best-case scenario, it's not always realistic, and you should ask your mentors and other key people (teachers, supervisors, etc.) to become advocates on your behalf. This is part of networking. Networking is a word many people use to describe the process of meeting people. The process could be as simple as getting someone's contact information or as deep as maintaining a lifelong friendship. For us, networking is about building relationships. Certainly, some relationships will be deeper than others; nevertheless, a relationship is more valuable than a one-time contact.

In the application process your networking will be beneficial. A letter of recommendation from a teacher who has known you for three years is a good example of a deep relationship. While not as deep, another example of good networking and building a relationship is contacting and meeting the admissions staff of the institution you would like to attend after high school. This contact can be built into a relationship through e-mails about your interest, a personal visit to campus, and asking for advice about applying, housing, tuition costs, etc. Be sure to start building this relationship before your senior year of high school!

LEARN. Janelle is a friend of ours who received great direction from her mentors regarding the college application process. She lived in Pennsylvania and started the college search process in eighth grade. It first started out as fun trips with her parents to nearby community colleges and universities. The desire to learn more about other schools grew, and anytime Janelle's family would travel to another state, they would stop at the well-known universities for a tour or at least to walk around for a while. Her family also loved football, so Janelle would study teams who came to play in her town and would find out more about their schools.

When it came time to apply for college, Janelle applied to 15 different institutions. The whole process of applying took her about a month, but she ended up with 7 offers to well-known universities. Her application highlighted her passion for, and involvement in, education. She was in several teaching societies and clubs and worked as a student teacher and volunteer in the local elementary school. Her GPA was high, and combined with her test scores, she did not have to come up with the funds to pay for tuition because of a scholarship. For the scholarship application, Janelle was able to request letters of recommendation on her behalf from several teachers with whom she worked closely and who were able to write about her skills and potential. When she was ready to submit everything, she did so in person and was remembered from her campus tour and e-mail communications. Janelle is a great example of how to manage the application process for college admissions and scholarships.

REFLECT. Please take as much time as you need to ponder the following questions, and with the help of your parents/mentors, fill in your answers in the space provided.

What type of research would you need to start doing now for your future college search process?

_____

_____

Why do you think it is important to meet people in person before applying for something like college admissions, scholarships, or jobs?

_____

_____

How many schools could you realistically apply to for college, and which ones would they be?

_____

_____

What are typical admissions and scholarship deadlines for schools near you?

_____

_____

What attributes and experiences make you unique?

_____

_____

Who do you know who would write you a positive letter of recommendation?

_____

_____

The Application Process

ACTION:

Take time to document your findings as you start to research the various colleges, universities, and other educational institutions that interest you. Collecting this information will help you narrow down your options based on what is most important to you, such as location, cost of attendance, and scholarship opportunities.

Please visit www.beatthemiddle.com/act to download this template.

COLLEGE APPLICATION PREPARATION SHEET

Insitution	Location	Deadlines for Admissions & Scholarships	General Admissions Requirements	Contact Info	Costs
1.					
2.					
3.					
4.					
5.					

Example on Back…

APPLICATION PROCESS EXAMPLE:

COLLEGE APPLICATION PREPARATION SHEET

Insitution	Location	Deadlines for Admissions & Scholarships	General Admissions Requirements	Contact Info	Costs
1. Dixie State University – dixie.edu	Saint George, Utah	Admissions August 1st Scholarships March 1st	No minimum GPA or test scores required Students average 3.2 GPA and 20 on ACT	435.652.777	$35 application fee $2,145 full-time resident tuition and fees
2. University of Nevada Las Vegas – unlv.edu	Las Vegas, Nevada	Admissions July 1st Scholarships February 1st	Need a 3.0 minimum weighted GPA Need a 22 or higher on ACT	702.774.8658	$60 application fee $7,147 full-time, non-resident tuition and fees
3. Stanford University – stanford.edu	Stanford, California	Admissions January 2nd Scholarships January 2nd	75% of admitted students have a 4.0 GPA 87% of admitted students have between a 30 and 36 on the ACT	650.723.3058	$90 application fee $14,373 full-time, non-resident tuition and fees
4. University of California Los Angeles – ucla.edu	Los Angeles, California	Admissions November 30th Scholarships May 1st	Average 3.93 weighted GPA Average ACT score of 29	310.825.3101	$70 application fee $2,962 full-time, non-resident tuition and fees
5. Southern Utah University – suu.edu	Cedar City, Utah	Admissions April 1st Scholarships December 1st	Must have an index score of 90+ - see site for details	435.586.7741	$50 application fee $2,962 full-time resident tuition and fees

The information gathered in the above table came from each school's website and is subject to change.

CONVERSATION 11:

INTERVIEWING

"Luck favors the prepared."

—*Dr. Louis Pasteur*

LISTEN. Whether for an internship, for a scholarship, or for a job, interviews are intimidating but important. Interviewing is developmental—you get better with practice. There are a couple types of interviews. The typical interview we all think of is a high-stress situation where interviewees are trying to convince a person or a group of people that they are ready and qualified for whatever is at stake, such as a job. For this type of interview, we offer some basic tips including:

- Research the organization thoroughly beforehand (you should understand the strategic direction and most everything on the website).

- Dress appropriately and be aware of your body language (it's always better to dress more professionally than you think you need to).

- Be confident and enjoyable to be around (organizations always look for those who fit into their culture).

- Address the person(s) interviewing you by name (try to write them down—whether beforehand or during the interview).

- Avoid lengthy responses to questions (be short and to the point—practice out loud).

- Use select accomplishments and experiences (have them memorized beforehand).

- Ask smart questions (previously researched).

- Connect with the organization (establish relationships before, during, and after your interview).

- Recognize others (properly thank those who helped with the interview process—parents/mentors, administrative assistants, interviewers, etc.).

These tips do not cover everything you will need to know to interview well. Other people have written entire books about this topic; nevertheless, we felt it necessary you understand the basics at a young age. Keep in mind there are professionals at your school and in the community who can prepare you for interviewing. A word of caution: when you receive many opinions about presenting yourself in an interview, you may get overwhelmed and lose sense of who you are. At some point you need to decide which advice is best for you personally and how to act accordingly because you will be more comfortable if you speak from your heart. You will smile more and have a pleasant demeanor that will come across as natural and welcoming. Be yourself and be honest in your answers. If you need more time to think about your answer, then ask your interviewer for a moment to think. A delayed, well-thought-out answer is much better than saying the first thing that comes to your mind. Also, if you are asked about a skill you don't have, be honest but indicate you are willing to do what it takes to acquire the skill.

Another type of interview is one where you seek out a specific individual with whom you would like to meet and either learn about the work he or she does and/or ask for potential job or internship opportunities. For example, if you want to work at a law firm one day, understanding what a lawyer does and connecting with one at a local firm is important. You can do this by going to a website, asking around, or directly calling a company. This process can be intimidating, but almost every professional we know is willing to help young students. As you go through this process, introduce yourself properly to the professional, and express your desire to learn. Do not ask for more than a simple, 20-minute conversation, and wait to see where it goes from there. Be sure to express gratitude for the time spent with you and carefully manage your future relationship.

These types of interviews are called informational interviews. We recommend doing them frequently. They can be with business owners, alumni of a college you're interested in attending, family members, neighbors, etc. Most people are flattered when you want to talk to them about their accomplishments and learn from their experiences. It makes them feel valued because you sincerely respect the work they do.

Remember, interviewing is developmental. As you interview, you will get better. Start practicing now by increasing the amount of face-to-face time you spend with those around you. Technology is crushing this important life skill, and we worry about you, our young friends, being able to become effective interpersonal communicators. We know you can use technology to better our world, but please do not forget the value of looking someone in the eye and having a meaningful conversation.

LEARN. We want to tell you about Larry, a person Blake interviewed one time for a scholarship. When Larry came into his interview, he was not a new face. He had interacted with several other students online and showed a genuine interest in the program.

This interaction established a solid first impression. Additionally, when Blake received Larry's résumé, he could tell it was detailed and well written.

Larry walked into the interview with a smile on his face, dressed in a suit, and introduced himself. As Larry sat down, he didn't appear to be nervous. He was engaged in the interview, and Blake could see this because of the way he sat and the way he listened intently to the questions. He was prepared for each question and gave brief, direct responses, highlighting his experiences and abilities with confidence. Larry was not afraid to show his sense of humor and was comfortable, yet maintained a professional image.

When asked a particularly difficult question, Larry asked Blake if he could take a second to think about his response. He then took out a folder, flipped through some notes, and gave a well-thought-out answer. When Blake asked Larry if he had any questions, he revealed his research about the scholarship and asked the questions he had prepared. After Larry's performance, clearly he was the right candidate for the scholarship.

REFLECT. Please take as much time as you need to ponder the following questions, and with the help of your parents/mentors, fill in your answers in the space provided.

What scares you most about interviews?

_____

_____

How can you and your parents/mentors practice for interviews?

_____

_____

Who would you like to have informational interviews with?

_____

_____

What accomplishments do you have, or want to have, to help you answer an interview question?

_____

_____

What experiences do you have, or want to have, to help you answer an interview question?

_____

_____

What interviewing resources are available to you?

_____

_____

11

CONVERSATION

Interviewing

ACTION:

As you begin to have informational and professional interviews, it is nice to be prepared beforehand. The sections below can be filled in prior to an interview. Use these notes to aid you in effectively answering interview questions. Be sure to thank your interviewers and anyone who helped you schedule the interview.

Please visit www.beatthemiddle.com/act to download this template.

INTERVIEW PREPARATION

Job Description	
Names of interviewers	
Research	
Requirements (basic and preferred)	
Matching strengths w/ requirements	
Weaknesses to address if asked	
Related experiences	
Questions for committee	
People to thank	

Example on Back…

CONVERSATION

BEAT
THE
MIDDLE

INTERVIEWING EXAMPLE:

INTERVIEW PREPARATION

Job description	Intern — Riverton Community Theatre Hiring a part-time intern to help with summer productions of "Wizard of Oz" and "The Pale Pink Dragon"
Names of interviewers	Rashida Jones, Director David Odette, Stage Manager
Research	Riverton Community Theatre performed "Oliver" and "The Phantom of the Opera" last year Rashida Jones has been the director for three years David Odette is new this year Most plays are sold out; however, attendance is decreasing and budgets are tight according to people I've talked to in past plays
Requirements (basic and preferred)	Basic — free time after school, available during most practices and all productions Preferred — background and interest in theater, music, and dance
Matching strengths w/ requirements	Basic — free in the summers and each production day; great planning skills Preferred — member of the drama club at school and taking piano lessons; also I am around many young people who I could market to
Weaknesses to address if asked	I'm a little young and inexperienced, but I have the desire and potential to contribute for at least a few years
Related experiences	I've been in two school plays, one of which I was the lead role; I am in the drama club and take theatre classes at school; Talk about the time I had to sing without a microphone or the time I forgot my lines and improvised and nobody could tell
Questions for committee	What are the top three things an intern could do to be valuable? How do they help their interns learn more about a career in acting?
People to thank	Rashida - interviewer, David - interviewer, Mike - assistant

CONVERSATION 12:

GIVING BACK

"Cultivate the habit of being grateful for every good thing that comes to you, and to give thanks continuously. And because all things have contributed to your advancement, you should include all things in your gratitude."

—*Ralph Waldo Emerson*

LISTEN. Well, we have reached the last conversation and, in our opinion, the most important. We have mentioned throughout this book that continually giving back is a necessary component of academic success. The eleven previous conversations are designed to increase your desire to act upon factors that contribute to academic success, as seen in the Academic Success Model. As you are held accountable to yourself and to your parents/mentors in learning and applying the factors of academic success over time, you will be presented with many opportunities to help others achieve their potential. Do not overlook these opportunities. Small and large acts of kindness go a long way.

Achieving academic success requires the help of others, and it is important you recognize when you are being helped. One type of recognition is a handwritten thank-you note. Never underestimate its power! It sounds like such a simple act and it is. For example, let's say you received help from your aunt in preparing a science fair project. We are pretty sure she wouldn't charge you for her time because she loves you and wants to help you. This is perfect because, as a student, you don't have the money to pay for this help; however, a handwritten thank-you note is all you need. She will feel valued and appreciate your kindness. When writing thank-you notes, be specific and thoughtful. Mail the note or take it to the recipient in a timely manner. People don't expect this type of recognition, so it makes the gesture very rewarding.

Another form of giving back when someone helps you is recognizing his or her efforts with some sort of gift. Be thoughtful with the gift by paying attention to clues. For example, if your teacher writes you a letter of recommendation and you happen to know he loves fishing, then maybe a fishing-themed gift would be appropriate to express your gratitude. Give simple, thoughtful gifts that are not out of your price range. Gifts are not something people expect, so anything you give is a surprise.

Just spending time with someone and listening is a powerful way of giving back. Follow the same steps in each conversation of this book—listen, learn, reflect, and act. Giving back is also about sharing what you feel and have learned through certain experiences. The ultimate academic success is not the fact that you personally achieved it. The ultimate academic success is reached when you inspire and help another person achieve his or her potential, and this is done most effectively as you reflect upon your own journey to academic success.

LEARN. This is the only conversation where we are not going to provide you an example of someone who gave back. We would like to try a little experiment. Who gave you this book? Be honest . . . we know you most likely didn't rush out to buy it yourself. Write a thank-you note to this person and see what happens to your relationship with them. You will not regret it. Instead of our giving you a story to read, you are writing your own.

REFLECT. Please take as much time as you need to ponder the following questions, and with the help of your parents/mentors, fill in your answers in the space provided.

How do you personally see yourself recognizing someone else?

_____

_____

How do you think other people feel when they are recognized?

_____

_____

Who are you currently not recognizing that you should be?

_____

_____

How will your own life be affected if you recognize others more?

_____

_____

What happened when you tried the experiment in the Learn section of this conversation?

_____

_____

What does ultimate academic success mean to you?

_____

_____

Giving Back

ACTION:

Always strive to recognize the efforts of those who assist you in your journey to academic success and look for personal opportunities to help others. Keep detailed notes of ways to express your gratitude for those who support you (write a note, send a gift, make a phone call, visit together, etc.) and act upon your ideas. In addition, dedicate time to help mentor others (tutoring, advising, volunteering, serving, etc.).

Please visit www.beatthemiddle.com/act to download this template.

GIVING BACK

Name	Title	Contact Info	Action	Notes

Example on Back...

CONVERSATION

GIVING BACK EXAMPLE:

GIVING BACK

Name	Title	Contact Info	Action	Notes
Rashida Jones	Director, Riverton Community Theatre	123 Thespian Way, Riverton, UT 84065	Thank-you note for interview	Rashida wanted an intern to be passionate about a career in theatre
Sam	Best Friend	Next-door Neighbor	Helped him with math homework	Get him a calculator
Ms. Kinzer	Advisor, National Honor Society	RHS Room 141, 12300 S. 2700 W., Riverton, UT, 84065	Thank-you gift for writing me a letter of recommendation	She loves lapel pins
Mom	Mom	My house	Birthday card	Her birthday is Friday

CONCLUDING THOUGHTS

Thank you for taking the time to read *Beat the Middle*. As we've presented the 12 factors of academic success to other middle school students and parents/mentors, it has been rewarding to see the excitement in their demeanor. A light turns on that wasn't there before. We are confident you, too, are excited about academic success and have a desire to achieve it together. We understand you may feel a bit overwhelmed; however, these feelings are natural and much better than the feelings you will have later if you do not prepare for higher education now.

In order to organize everything we've discussed throughout this book, we've created a Student Guide that lists the main points you learned from each conversation. Use your guide as a checklist of progress. We've also included an example for your reference.

Your Summary Guide

01
Goals and Mentors
❑

❑

❑

02
Planning and Preparation
❑

❑

❑

03
Time Management
❑

❑

❑

04
GPA
❑

❑

. ❑

05
College Entrance Exams
❑

❑

❑

06
Internships and Work Experience
❑

❑

❑

07
Extra- and Co-Curricular Activities
❑

❑

❑

08
Service
❑

❑

❑

09
Money Management and Scholarships
❑

❑

❑

10
The Application Process
❑

❑

❑

11
Interviewing
❑

❑

❑

12
Giving Back
❑

❑

❑

Please visit www.beatthemiddle.com/act to download this template.

Example Summary Guide

01
Goals and Mentors

- Always keep an updated list of your top six life goals
- Make sure your goals are detailed
- Utilize parents/mentors

02
Planning and Preparation

- Set aside time to plan and prepare daily
- Plan ahead – especially for the next six months
- Don't forget to research, research, research...and then plan

03
Time Management

- Utilize your preferred time management tool
- Keep an organized to-do list
- Use reminders and write down important dates and deadlines

04
GPA

- Your GPA is based on hard work – always track it
- Never, ever cheat
- Take time when selecting classes and teachers

05
College Entrance Exams

- Don't wait to take the exam without practicing
- Don't get frustrated with low scores, keep trying as long as it takes
- Take the ACT/SAT at least three times before your senior year of high school

06
Internships and Work Experience

- Start thinking about what career and lifestyle you desire
- Build a résumé and constantly update it
- Represent yourself professionally both in person and online

07
Extra- and Co-Curricular Activities

- Get involved in both extra- and co-curricular activities
- The more diverse you are the better – do what is fun and relevant for your goals
- Avoid wasting time – don't be lazy – be anxiously engaged

08
Service

- Never underestimate the value of volunteering and serving others
- Consider starting a club or group that you're passionate about
- Find ways to build your leadership experience through service

09
Money Management and Scholarships

- Create and continually use a personal income statement
- Do not spend more than you make and start the habit of saving money regularly
- Research scholarship opportunities at schools and other organizations

10
The Application Process

- Identify the top five institutions you could see yourself attending after high school
- Understand the application process and deadlines at the institutions you want to attend
- It is very beneficial to visit campuses and meet people in person before applying

11
Interviewing

- Frequently seek out opportunities to conduct informational interviews
- Utilize the professional career services and interviewing resources around you
- Be prepared (research, professionalism, practice, memorized experiences, etc.)

12
Giving Back

- True success is not just personal achievement but also occurs when you help others achieve their potential
- Notes and small gifts are good ways to recognize others
- You will personally benefit the more you give back and recognize others

Please visit www.beatthemiddle.com/act **to download this template.**

In closing, we would like to leave students with the words of Walt Disney, "If you can dream it, you can do it!" For parents/mentors, we want you to keep in mind something Tyler Perry once said, "There are some folks you can talk to until you're blue in the face—they're never going to get it and they're never going to change. But every once in a while, you'll run into someone who is eager to listen, eager to learn, and willing to try new things. Those are the people we need to reach. We have a responsibility as parents, older people, teachers, and people in the neighborhood to recognize that."

We assure you that as you follow the Academic Success Model together, you will beat the middle and help others do the same.

Blake and Bo

ABOUT BLAKE AND BO NEMELKA

Blake and Bo grew up in Utah where they graduated from South Hills Middle School and Riverton High School. They continued their education together at Utah State University where they were selected to be student ambassadors and played for the university tennis team. The brothers each took a two-year hiatus in their education to serve as missionaries for their faith. Blake served in Lima, Peru, and Bo served in Merida, Mexico.

Upon their return, Blake and Bo continued their education at Utah State University while interning for the late Dr. Stephen R. Covey. They were both selected as Huntsman Scholars and graduated with honors from the Jon M. Huntsman School of Business. Blake later attended Vanderbilt University where he graduated with his master's degree in education administration, and Bo attended

Yale University where he graduated with his master's degree in healthcare management. Blake and Bo are each happily married with young children and continue their love for education in their personal and professional lives.